SYMBOLS AND TERMS OF THE CHURCH

Mark P. Bangert

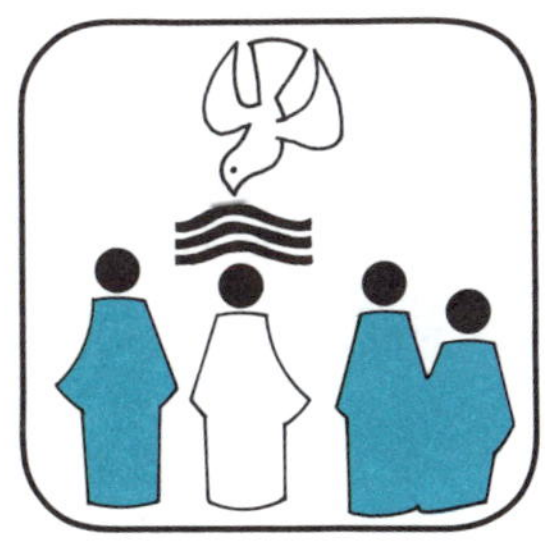

Augsburg Fortress, Minneapolis

CONTENTS

Symbols and Terms of the Church

Cover: Lecy Design
Inside design and illustration: Avis Benson

International Standard Book No. 0-8066-2522-8

Manufactured in the United States of America

PREFACE

The word *symbol*, of Greek origin, literally means "something that pulls together." A simple symbol is a representation limited to one basic element. Compound symbols are two or more simple symbols, combined for the purpose of elaborating the subject presented. Both of these have characteristics that will assist us in understanding their origins and uses:

- Symbols help us to *know fully.* A lamb that symbolizes Christ typifies lambs in general, so that we can grasp all those lamb-like actions and words of Jesus under a singular framework. Because symbols function best when they are versatile and capable of representing diverse experiences, their presentations are generally stylized.

- Because symbols pull together many experiences, they function as *carriers of feeling.* For a single individual the symbol of the cross may draw on feelings related to that symbol on wedding rings, as well as on a funeral pall used for burial. As carriers of feeling symbols thus evoke response.

- Symbols are *communal.* Symbols emerge from within groups and serve to bind such groups together. They enable communication on a wide level, opening up Christians to the experiences of the entire church.

- Symbols are what *make us human,* for as communal vehicles of feeling, experience, knowledge, and disclosure, they assist us in understanding and ordering the experiences of human life.

SIMPLE SYMBOLS

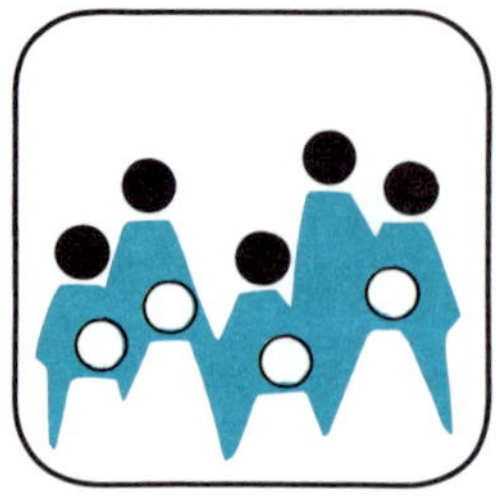

FOUNDATIONAL SYMBOLS

Foundational symbols are freeze frames that derive from the sacramental actions of the church and are central to Christian experience, evoking repeated involvement. In these sacramental experiences Christians encounter the presence of God in Christ.

Assembly

Jesus reminded the disciples he was present even when as few as two were gathered in his name. Any gathering then can be a symbol of the presence of God in the world. As it invokes the name of Jesus, such an assembly becomes a place where that presence is encountered.

Water

For Christians, water is a symbol of grace. Water is universally experienced as cleansing, purifying, life-giving, and sometimes destructive. In Baptism all of these meanings and uses come together as a Christian is led from death to life by means of water.

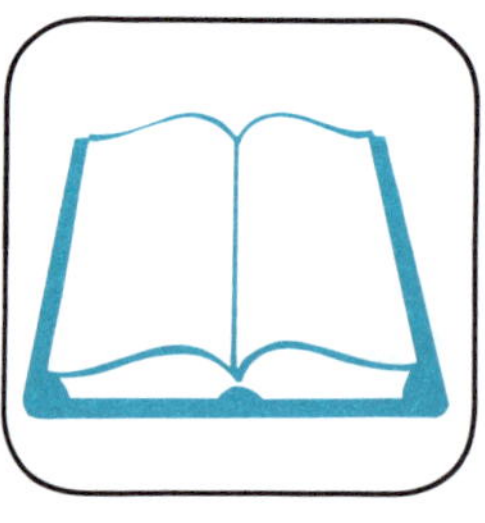

Bible

Scrolls, ancient manuscripts, and books are commonly believed to contain significant knowledge and are therefore symbols of wisdom. Foremost among Christians are the four Gospels because they contain the story and teaching of Jesus. The Bible, which contains these Gospels, therefore signifies Jesus as God's Word to people. The Bible is also the symbol of the power of the gospel, of the proclaimed and read Word, of the presence of Jesus, and of the commission to evangelize the world.

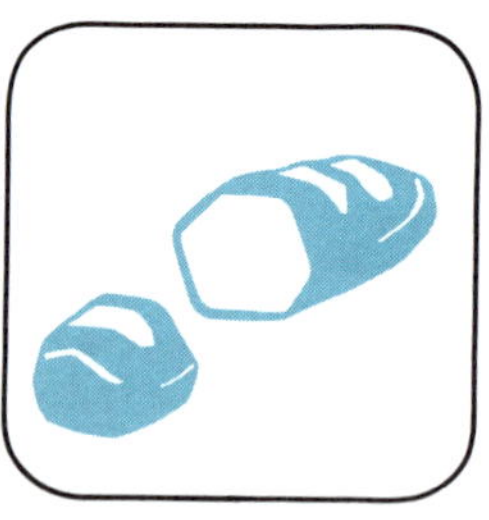

Bread

Bread is a symbol of nourishment, of Jesus, of the gift of salvation, and of the church. Long held as a staple of life and as a source of strength, bread is brought into existence through hard work and ample harvest. Its daily availability depends upon God so it symbolizes gift. In Holy Communion, bread as staple, strength, and gift manifests the presence of Christ. In the eating of this holy food believers are nourished by Jesus, the bread of life.

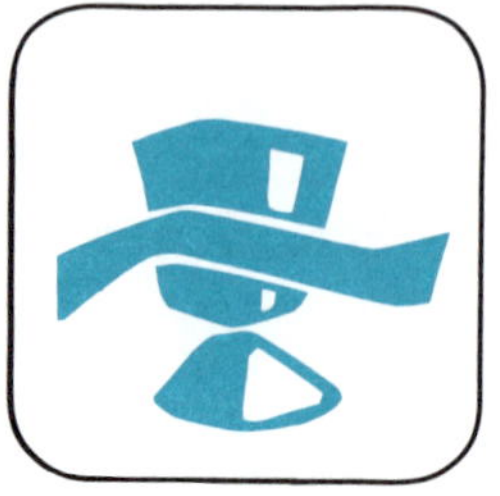

Wine

Wine symbolizes joy, conviviality, life, and suffering. In Holy Communion Jesus chose to use wine to symbolize the pouring out of himself in suffering and offering, just as grapes under pressure yield their juices. In Christian symbolism the wine or drinking of wine is usually transferred to depictions of the vine, grapes, or chalice.

CROSSES

The apostle Paul invited his readers to use the image of the cross as a way to sum up the gospel of God's saving power in Jesus Christ. In a short time the visual representation came to mean Jesus himself, his sacrificial death, and his victory over sin and death.

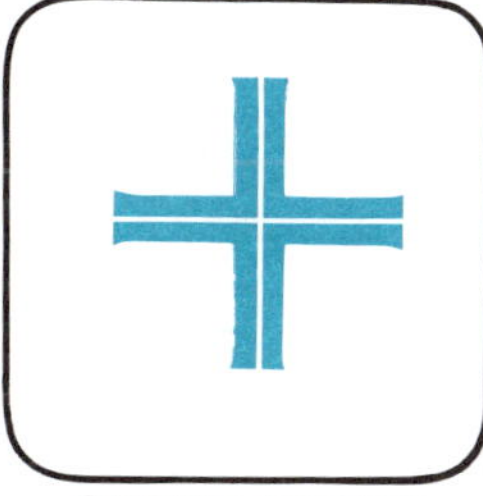

GREEK CROSS

Greek Cross • This form is distinguished by its four equal arms.

Latin Cross • The Latin cross, the traditional cross of Jesus' crucifixion, always has the lower vertical arm longer than any other. Sometimes the upper arm is shorter than, sometimes equal to, the horizontal arms.

DOUBLE CROSS

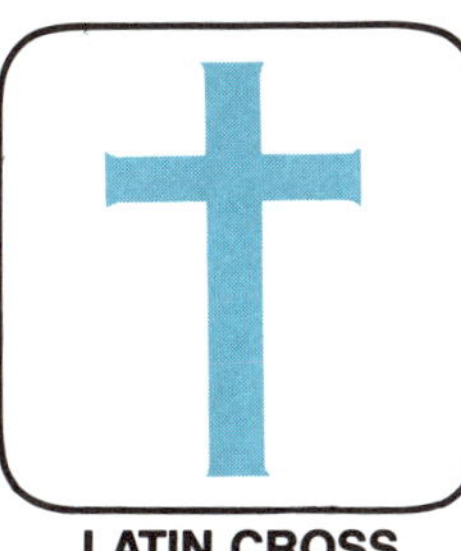

LATIN CROSS

Tau Cross • This form receives its name from the letter "T" ("Tau" in Greek), which is shaped this way in Greek and Latin. One tradition has it that on such a cross St. Philip was martyred.

St. Andrew's Cross • The name derives from a tradition that states that St. Andrew was martyred on a cross of this form.

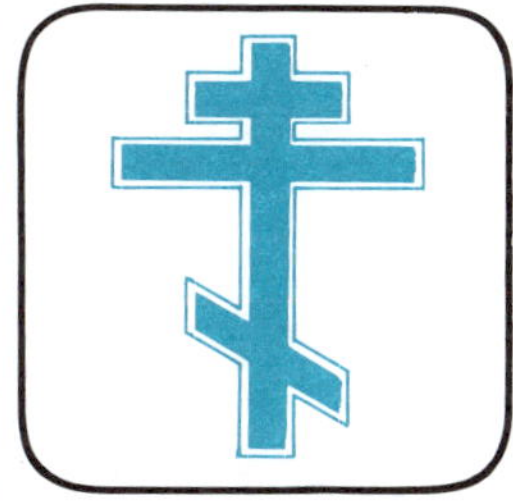

BYZANTINE CROSS

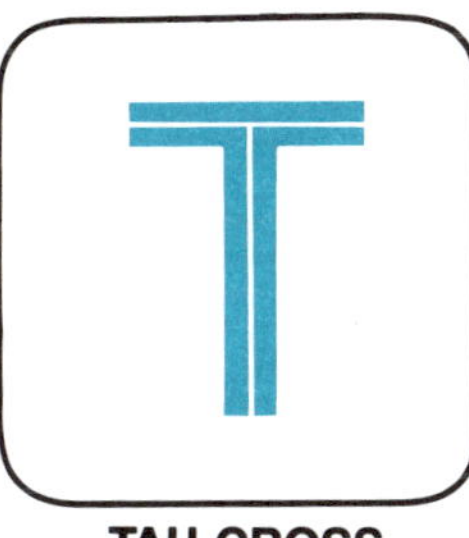

TAU CROSS

Double Cross • This form results from a Latin cross on which the Board of Inscription, the title placed over Jesus at his crucifixion, has been attached.

Byzantine or Russian Cross • Frequently used in Byzantine art, this form is the Double Cross with the addition of a footrest.

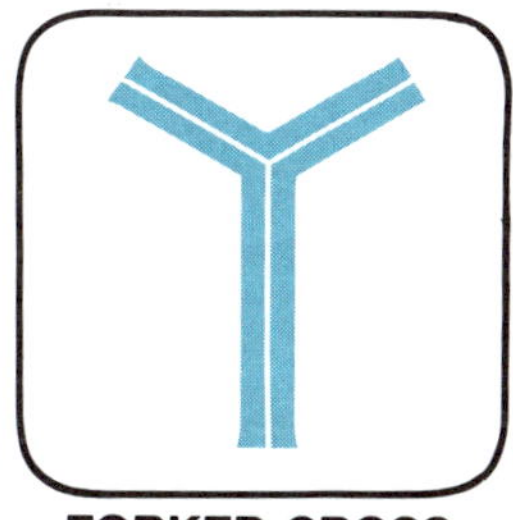

FORKED CROSS

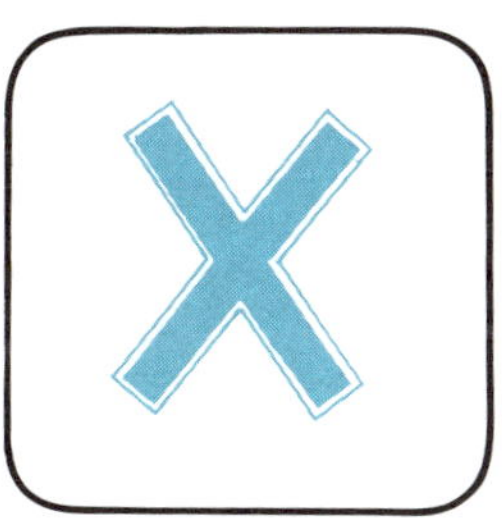

ST. ANDREW'S CROSS

Forked Cross • Known in the Middle Ages as a "thief's cross," this form suggests overtones of the Trinity. For some it stresses the prayer aspects of Christ's suffering since the arms simulate arms lifted in prayer.

Papal Cross • This is a double cross with the addition of another horizontal arm.

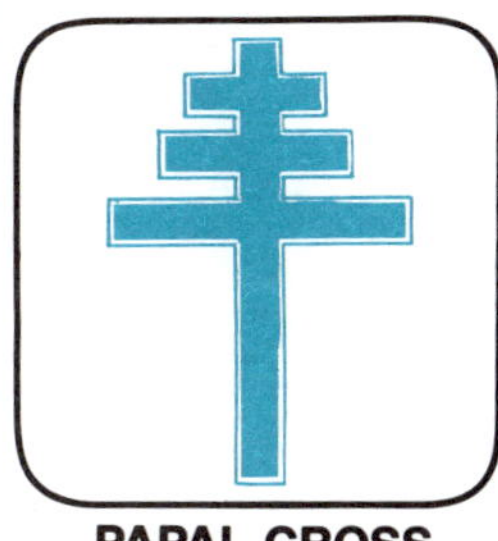

PAPAL CROSS

RING CROSS

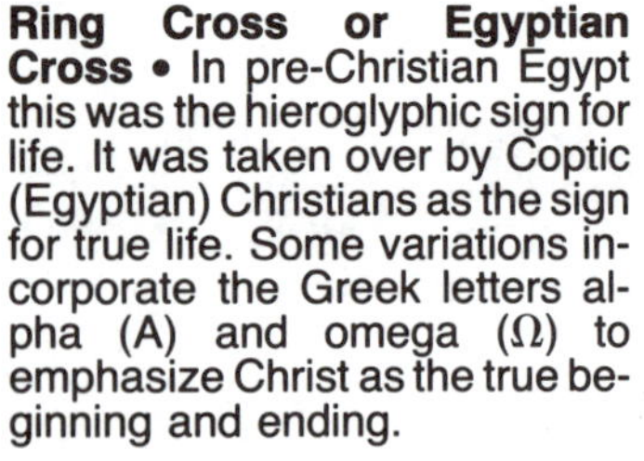

Ring Cross or Egyptian Cross • In pre-Christian Egypt this was the hieroglyphic sign for life. It was taken over by Coptic (Egyptian) Christians as the sign for true life. Some variations incorporate the Greek letters alpha (A) and omega (Ω) to emphasize Christ as the true beginning and ending.

MALTESE CROSS

Multiple Cross • This form results from the combination of four Latin crosses and suggests the four corners of the world over which Jesus reigns.

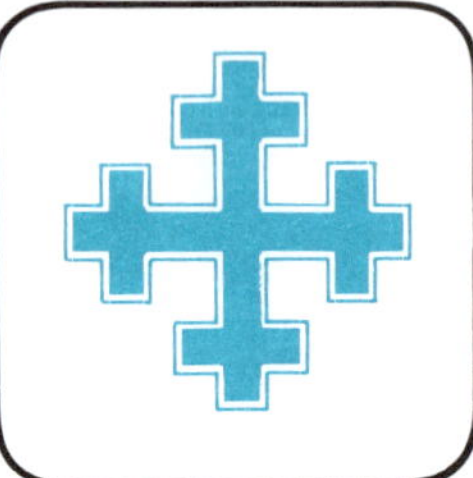

MULTIPLE CROSS

ANCHOR CROSS

Crutch Cross • A form of the cross developed from four Tau crosses, each arm also resembling a crutch.

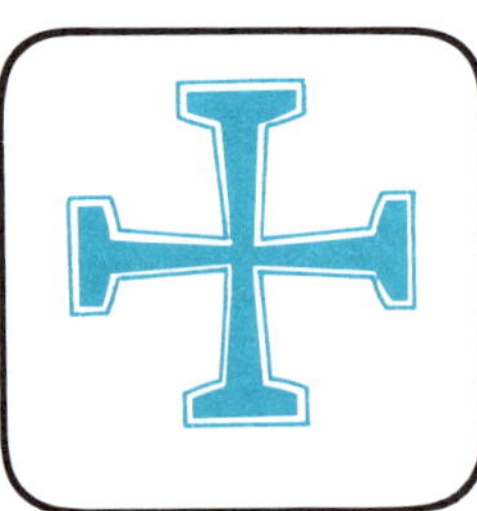

CRUTCH CROSS

Jerusalem Cross or Pilgrim's Cross • The addition of four small crosses to a Greek cross suggests in sum the five wounds of Christ. It was a favorite emblem of eleventh- and twelfth-century pilgrims visiting Jerusalem.

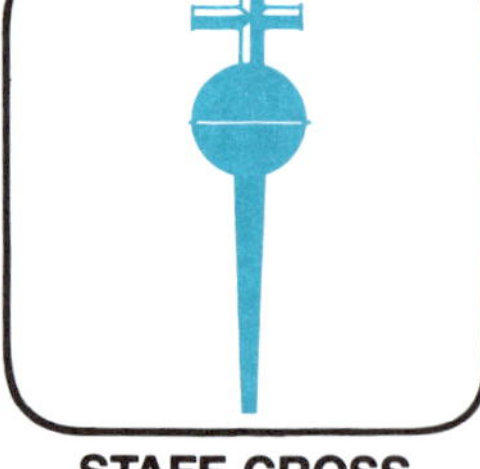

STAFF CROSS

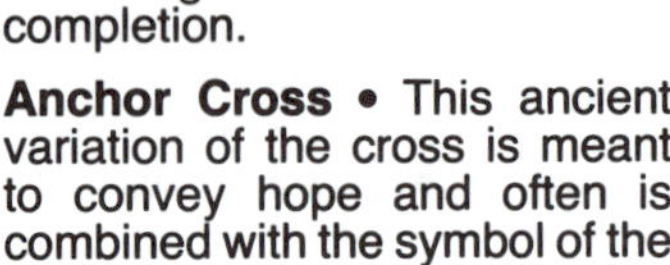

Maltese Cross • This cross is distinguished by its eight points, which together mean fullness or completion.

Anchor Cross • This ancient variation of the cross is meant to convey hope and often is combined with the symbol of the fish.

Staff Cross • A cross at the end of a staff indicates authority, especially if it is jeweled or adorned with precious metals. Placed in an upright position, it conveys the authority of Christ's reign in a particular place or in the whole world.

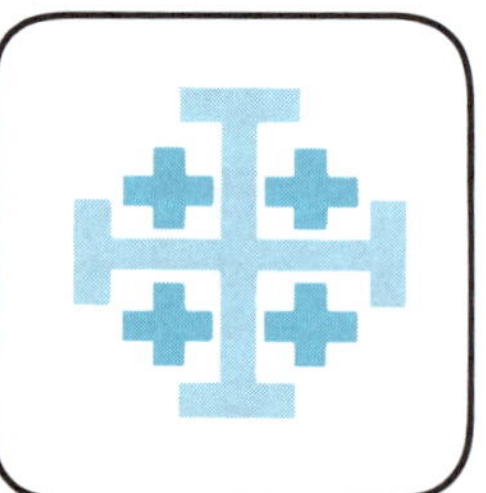

JERUSALEM CROSS

FOUR EVANGELISTS

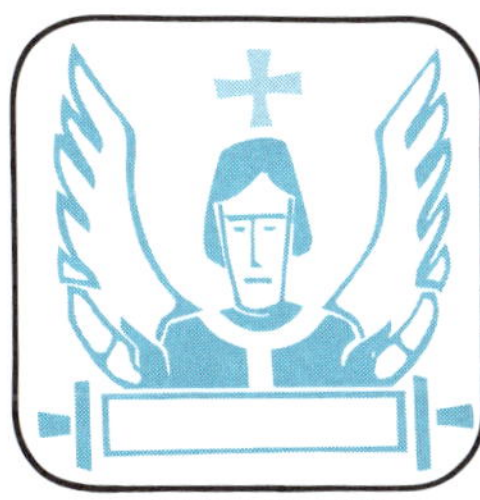

MATTHEW

Matthew is depicted as a human or angel, because his gospel stresses the genealogy and humanity of Christ.

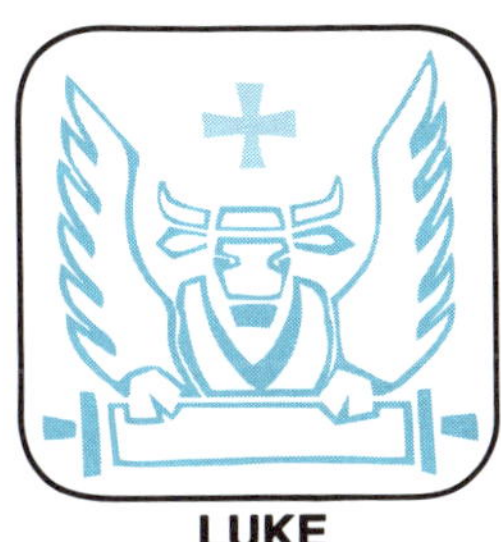

LUKE

Mark, represented by a lion, lifts up the royal divinity and resurrection of Jesus.

Luke, seen as an ox, accents the sacrificial nature of Jesus.

MARK

John, whose gospel soars into the wisdom of God and mirrors the ascension, is presented as an eagle.

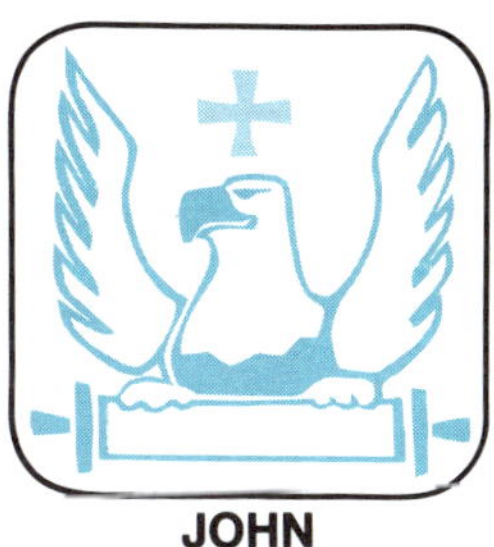

JOHN

The symbols for each usually include one or more sets of wings.

LETTERS

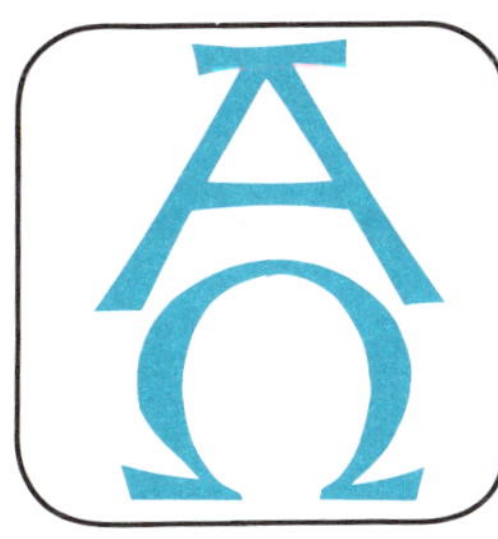

ALPHA AND OMEGA
In the Greek alphabet alpha is the first letter and omega the last. Upper case forms are used most frequently as symbols for Jesus identified as the first and the last.

I/IOTA
In Greek the letter iota is the same as "i" and is the first letter of the name of Jesus.

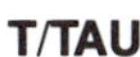

T/TAU
This Greek letter is in the shape of a cross and therefore represents Christ and the crucifixion.

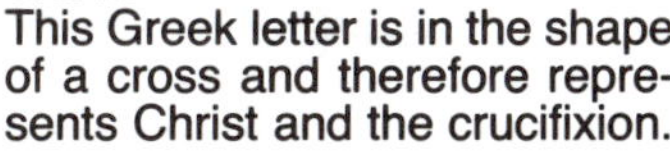

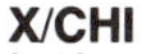

X/CHI
In the Greek alphabet this letter is the first letter of the word for Christ. It is usually employed with other letters to form monograms.

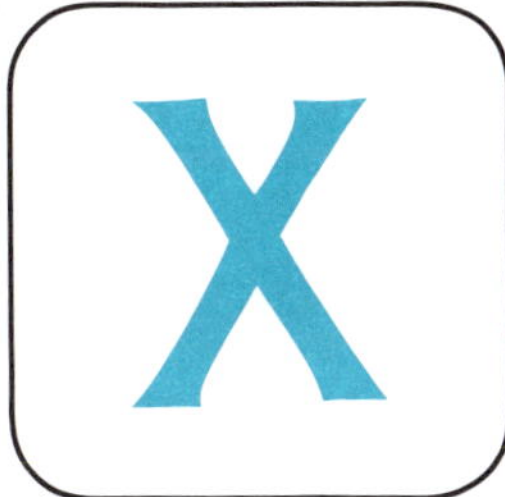

MONOGRAMS

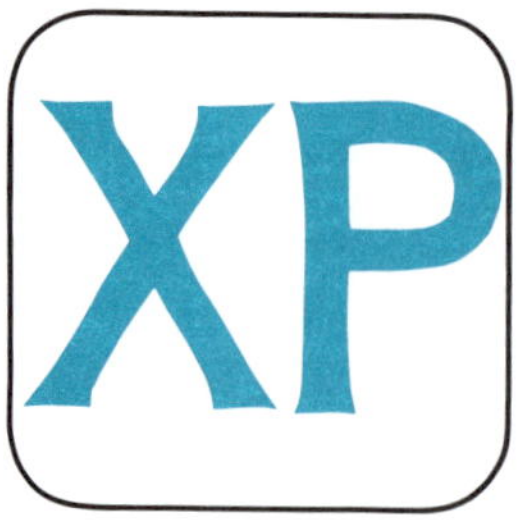

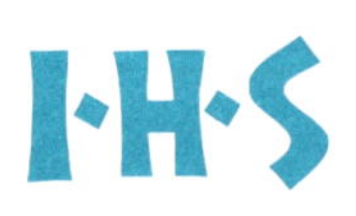

CHI-RHO
Chi and Rho are the first two letters of the Greek word for Christ.

CHI-IOTA
Chi is the first letter of the Greek word for Christ and iota is the first letter of the Greek word for Jesus.

IC XC NIKA
Iota with C is shorthand for the Greek word for Jesus. Chi with C, or S, denotes the Greek word for Christ. Both used with the Greek NIKA, which means "conquers," thus mean: Jesus Christ conquers.

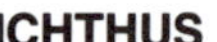

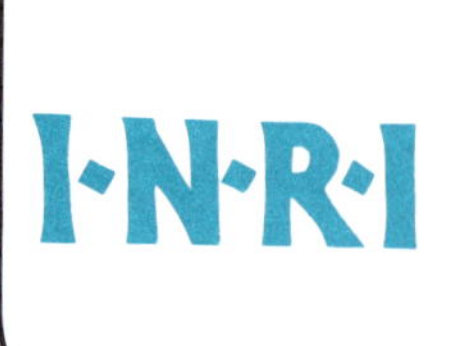

ICHTHUS
This is the Greek word for fish. As a monogram it originates from the first letters of five names for Jesus: Ι, Iesus; Χ, Christos; Θ, Theos; Υ, Uios; Σ, Soter.

IHS
Another popular variation of the first letters of Jesus' name in Greek capitals is IHSOUS, IHS, or IHC, since S was sometimes written as C.

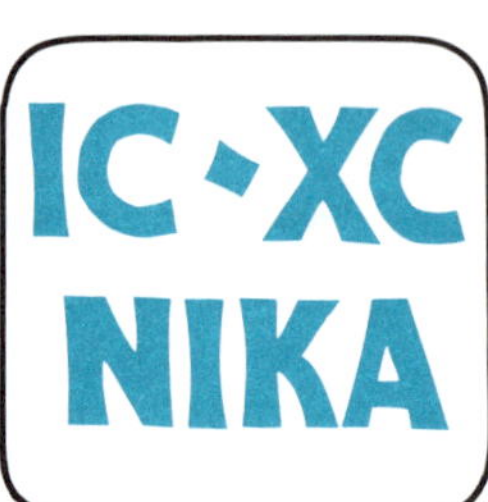

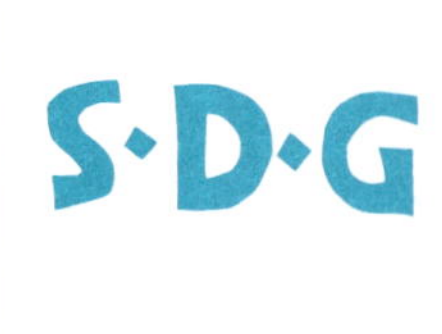

INRI
These are the first letters of the four Latin words *Iesus Nazarenus Rex Judaeorum* (Jesus of Nazareth, King of the Jews).

SDG
The first letters of the Latin words *Soli Deo Gloria* mean "To God alone be glory."

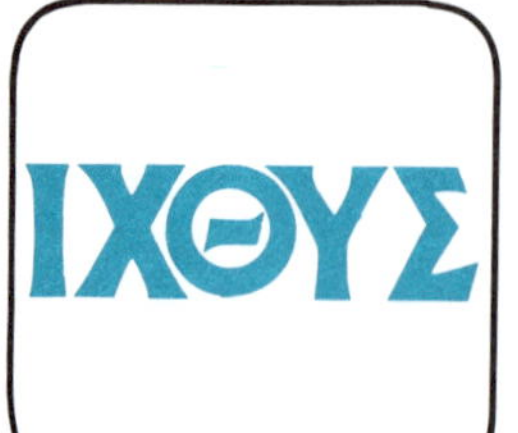

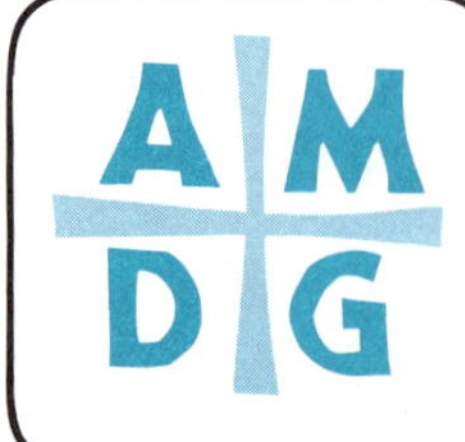

AMDG
These are the first letters of the four Latin words *Ad Majorem Dei Gloriam* (To the greater glory of God). The letters are frequently found inscribed on buildings or cornerstones.

GEOMETRIC FIGURES

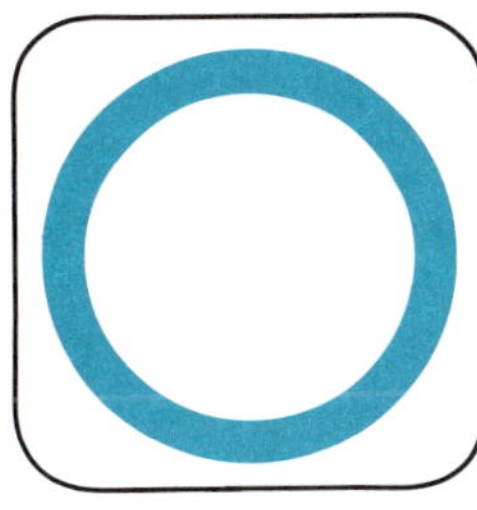

CIRCLE

Because it has no point of beginning or ending, the circle is an image of eternity or fullness. The circle also elicits the notion of equality since every point is equidistant from the center. Wheels as moving circles indicate never-ending motion and have been employed to represent the course of the sun (God's son), the year, and its seasons.

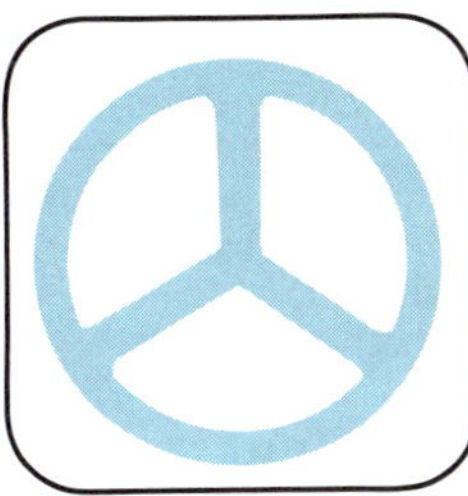

NIMBUS

The Latin word *nimbus* means cloud, which is what people often imagine as surrounding the appearance of a god-like being. Visually the nimbus appears as a circle, or halo, surrounding the head of a god or of a god-like person. Sometimes it is star-shaped, triangular (for God the Father), or rectangular (for someone still living). Three rays of light, or an equally segmented nimbus, sometime surround a symbol of a person of the Trinity. A nimbus implies glory, which is why the color of a nimbus is usually white or gold. When a nimbus surrounds the entire figure representing God or a saint it is called *aureole,* meaning "golden" or "glorious."

TRIANGLE

A triangle with equal sides suggests the Trinity. Usually the triangle is depicted with other symbols, such as a circle, the eye of God, a hand, or a dove.

TRIQUETRA

The triquetra, a symbol for the Trinity, is formed by three equal arcs that have been interwoven to suggest continuous flow. The points of the arcs are the points of an imagined equilateral triangle, another symbol of the Trinity.

BUTTERFLY
The butterfly is a symbol of the death and resurrection of Christ, and thus of any faithful Christian. In pre-Christian times it was understood to be a symbol of the soul, deriving its meaning from the three stages of a butterfly's life: caterpillar (life), chrysalis (death), and butterfly (resurrection).

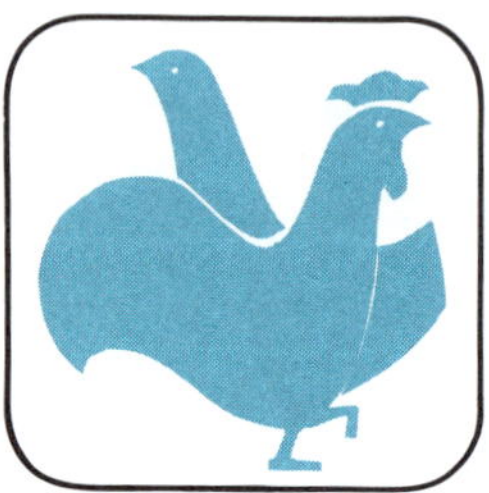

COCK, HEN
As the morning herald of light, the cock was an ancient symbol for the recurring victory of light over darkness. On weather vanes and peaks of church buildings the cock is meant to summon the faithful to prayer and repentance. Crowing cocks thus are also symbols of the ministry. The hen derives its symbolic significance from Jesus' reference to himself as the hen who gathers the faithful.

DOVE
The dove is the preeminent symbol for the Holy Spirit since, according to the evangelists, it was chosen to embody the Holy Spirit at Jesus' baptism. By extension the dove also symbolizes Pentecost. It is the means by which divine inspiration is depicted. Seven doves refer to the seven gifts of the spirit. A dove with an olive branch in its mouth recalls Noah and the ark and is meant to convey peace and forgiveness.

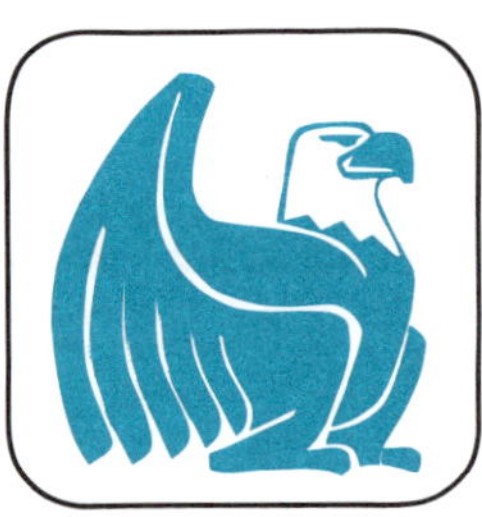

EAGLE
In pre-Christian cultures people were convinced that eagles flew to the sun in order to find new life and strength for their wings. Hence the eagle became a symbol for either life in Christ or for a Christian's personal ascension. As eagles take their young to the sun for fresh vistas of perception and understanding, so the eagle became a symbol for contemplation and discovery of the mysteries of God. St. John is represented by an eagle.

FISH
The fish was a common symbol for water but when combined with an anchor quickly became a symbol of baptism for Christians. Also, Jesus fed the hungry crowd with loaves and fish. Because many Christians understood this miracle as a form of Holy Communion, the fish is sometimes employed as a symbol for Holy Communion. *Ichthus,* the Greek word for fish, is comprised of the initials of Jesus, Christ, God, Son, Savior.

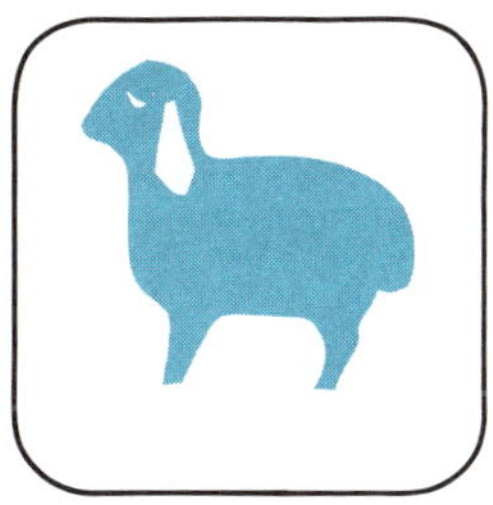

LAMB
Because of the Passover, the lamb and its blood have been recognized as signs of God's deliverance, later referring to Jesus, the Lamb of God, as the specific means of God's deliverance. The lamb, with a staff cross, is frequently presented with the four evangelists. Lambs can also symbolize Christians gathered as the church, with Jesus being the Good Shepherd.

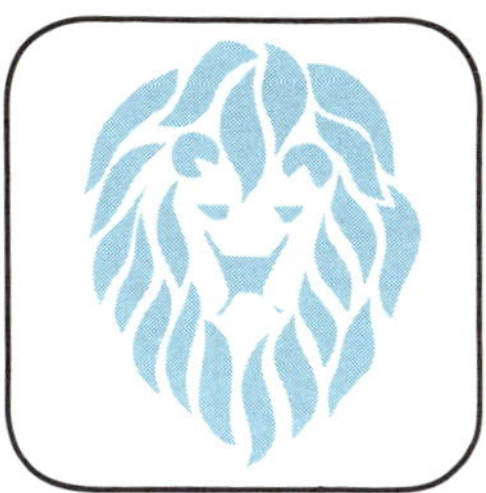

LION
The lion connotes strength and potential destruction. Among the more than one hundred metaphorical references in the Bible, many use the lion to generate a healthy fear of evil spirits who are bent on destroying the faithful. The lion is viewed as a protector of graves and of cities, and sometimes is associated with the resurrection. In some Christian art, Christ as lion seeks to destroy the dragon or devil. A lion is the symbol for St. Mark.

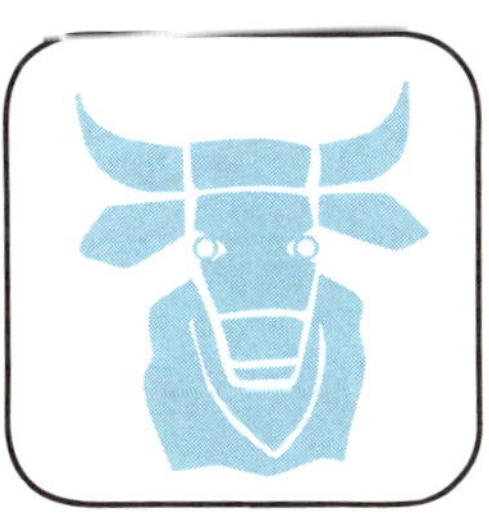

OX
Anciently the ox represented fruitfulness of the earth, presumably because of its use in tilling. It is also a symbol of sacrifice. In the Old Testament young offspring from the oxen family of animals were often sacrificed in cultic rituals, which led to Christian use of the ox as a symbol of Christ's sacrifice. St. Luke, the evangelist, is represented by an ox.

PHOENIX
The phoenix is a symbol for the resurrected Christ. According to Egyptian accounts the phoenix was thought to have a life span of nearly five hundred years. Then, at the close of its life, the phoenix would fly to Heliopolis in Egypt where it would burn itself on a funeral pyre. After three days it would rise from the ashes and return to its home.

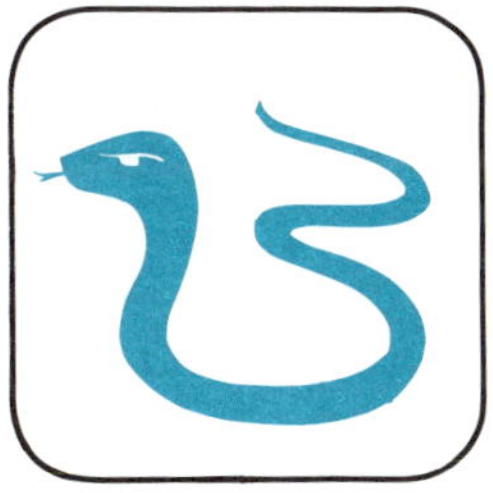

SNAKE, DRAGON
Because the serpent in the ancient story of human temptation and the fall has been interpreted as a snake, snakes symbolize temptation, evil, or the devil. Dragons, mythological beasts meant to induce terror of the worst kind, are often employed as substitutes for or equivalents of snakes.

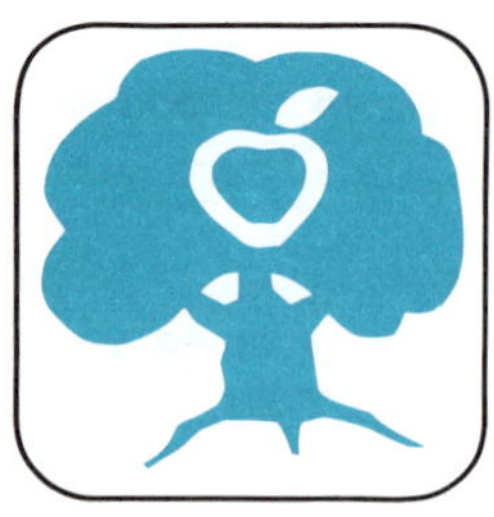

APPLE, APPLE TREE
A symbol of fruitfulness and beauty, the apple became a symbol for love. In the Song of Solomon one's lover is compared to a beautiful apple tree and to the shade it provides. The apple also has been assumed to be the fruit that Adam ate in the Garden of Eden. It is thus a symbol for sin and death.

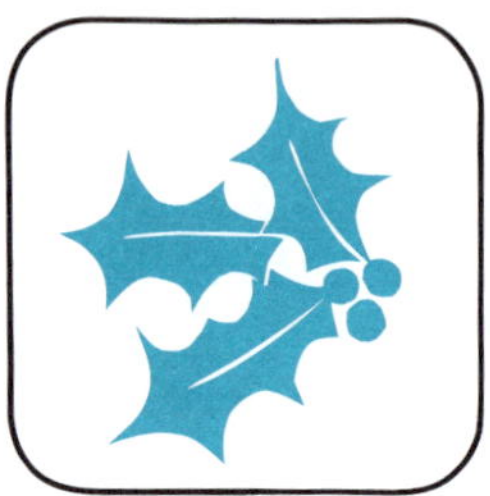

HOLLY OAK
The holly oak, an evergreen with thorny leaves and red berries, is a symbol for the passion of Christ. The thorns call to mind Christ's crown of thorns, and the red berries the shedding of blood. At Christmas it is common to arrange holly leaves in a wreath. The circle and leaves suggest eternal life and link Christ's incarnation, passion, and resurrection.

LILY
Jesus singled out the lily as a sign of faith in God's grace. White lilies used in conjunction with the Virgin Mary or other saints indicate meekness and purity, an accent derived from the Song of Solomon. The fleur-de-lis is a variety of lily and is meant to suggest royalty.

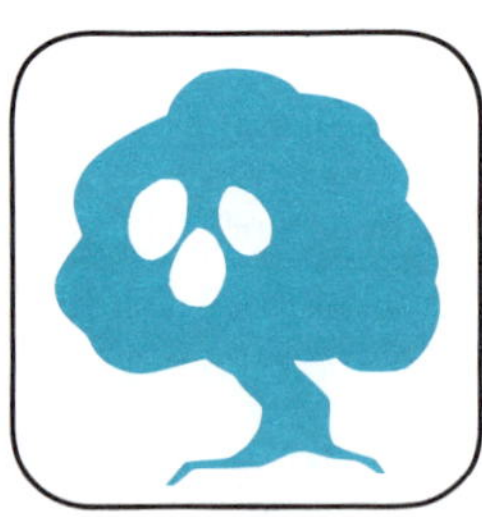

OLIVE TREE
Having leaves that are always green, the olive tree has long been a symbol of eternal life. In the Old Testament the olive tree represented the providence of God, God's blessing, grace, and divine wisdom. The olive branch symbolizes peace because it was what the dove brought back to the ark when the flood subsided. Olive oil, a symbol of the ampleness of grace.

PALM
The palm symbolizes life and victory. The tree of life from paradise has been thought by some to have been a palm tree. Palm branches were waved at victorious heroes.

ROSE
The rose means beauty and love, especially the beauty and love of martyrs whose blood the rose symbolizes. Some Christians use the white rose to represent purity, so it is often employed to symbolize the Virgin Mary, the "rose without thorns."

SEEDS
Because the seed is the juncture of the life cycle, it is a symbol of life and new life, of resurrection and hope. The mustard seed, in particular, symbolizes faith, and, because of the parable of the sower, seeds in general connote the Word of God.

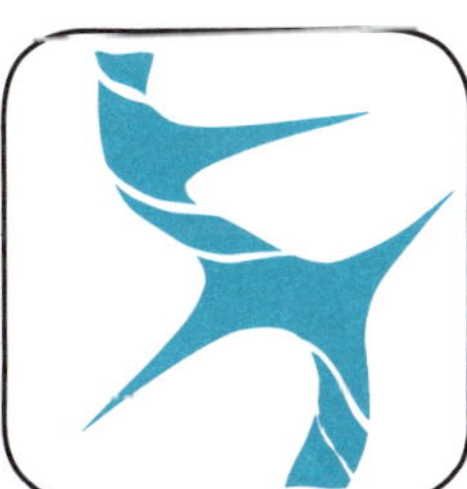

THORNS
Plentitude of thistles and thorns together with their troublesome nature for farmers and gardeners result in their use as a symbol for sin and toil.

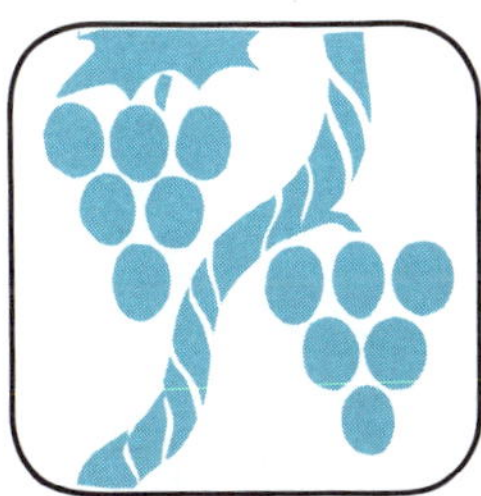

VINE, VINEYARD, GRAPES
Jesus identified himself as the true vine. The branches of that vine are a symbol of the church. In the New Testament, grapes and wine, both fruits from the vine, became a symbolic presentation of the gifts of grace available in Holy Communion. In the Old Testament, grape clusters were a sign of God's gracious providence. The people of Israel were encouraged to think of themselves as God's vineyard.

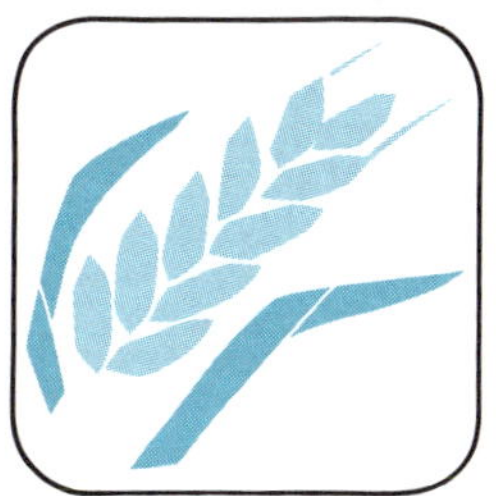

WHEAT
Grain or wheat demonstrates the life cycle of nature and thus is used to denote the life, death, and resurrection of Christ. Grain also means Holy Communion, since from the gathered grain bread is made.

FIRE, LIGHT, CANDLE

Primarily, fire accompanies an epiphany of God, such as in the burning bush, or symbolizes Christ's presence in the flame of the paschal candle on Easter Eve. Light produced by fire is a symbol of the pervading presence of God because the light of Christ vanquishes the darkness of sin and death. The Holy Spirit was embodied in flames, so the Spirit or the seven gifts of the Spirit are represented often as flames. Hearts aflame denote burning love, especially for God. Fire is also a symbol of purification, so it is associated with the testing of saints.

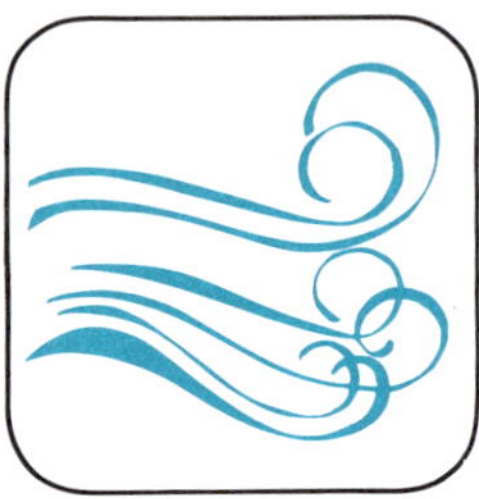

WIND

Wind symbolizes the breath of God. Being felt, not seen, sometimes directional, sometimes absent, wind has a mysterious and unpredictable character. Specifically it is a symbol of the Holy Spirit.

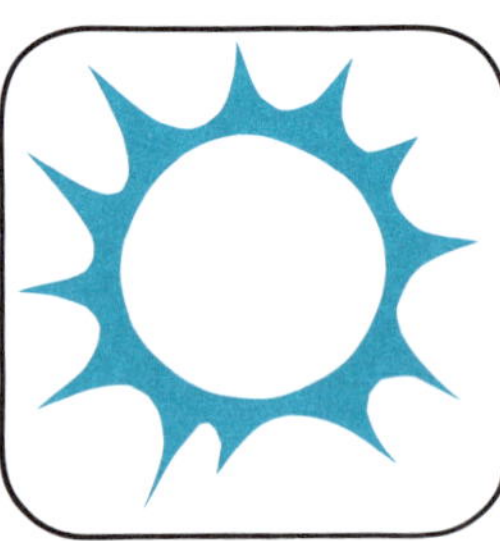

SUN, LIGHT

Christians took up the sun as a symbol for God; they faced east for prayer and built church buildings so worshipers could naturally look east in order to praise God. As Christians confessed Jesus to be God's Son, they thought of him also as the sun, but even more as the light of the world.

MOON

Because the sun became darkened at the crucifixion the sun and moon are sometimes chosen by artists to symbolize visually the effect of Jesus' death on all of creation. Sun and moon occasionally denote the Old and New Testaments, and also signal the destruction of the world. Because the phases of the moon include a "death," the moon also represents birth, death, and resurrection.

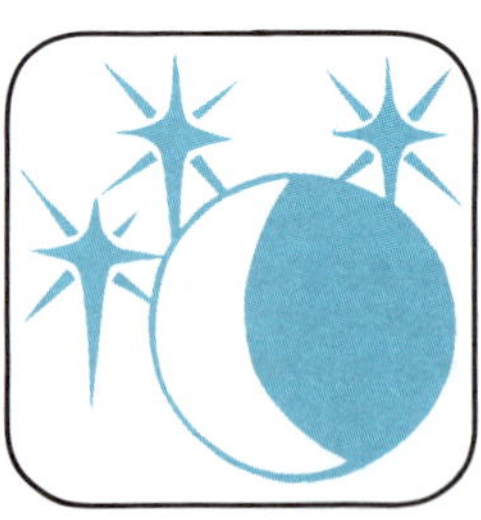

STARS

Together with the sun and moon the stars symbolize creation, especially creation's obedience to God since stars, it was thought, stayed where God put them. Stars also signify heaven in Christian art. A single bright star with a manger stands for the Star of Bethlehem and messianic fulfillment. Jesus the Messiah is known as the bright Morning Star. Seven stars refer to the angels of the seven congregations in Revelation. Twelve stars represent a crown for Mary, the heavenly woman, and a single star sometimes represents Mary as the Star of the Sea.

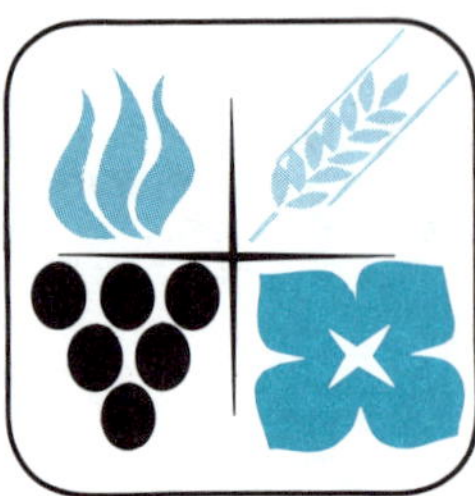

SEASONS

In Christian symbolism the four seasons are represented by blooms (spring), grain (summer), grapes (fall), and olives or fire for warmth (winter).

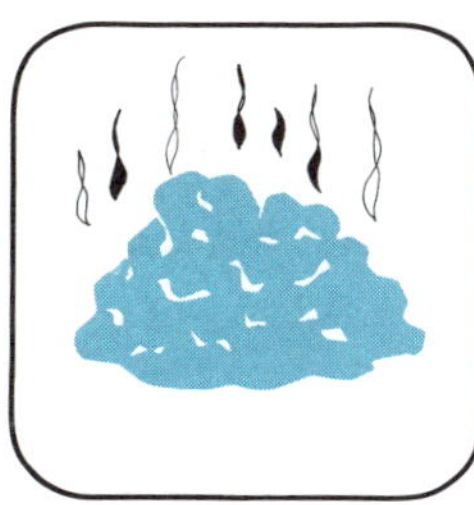

ASHES

The application of ashes to one's head or body was a sign of grief or penitence. Wearing ashes was a recognition of the nearness of death or destruction. Ashes, obtained by burning palms from the previous Palm Sunday, are often applied in liturgies for Ash Wednesday to remind worshipers of their own end and the end of all things.

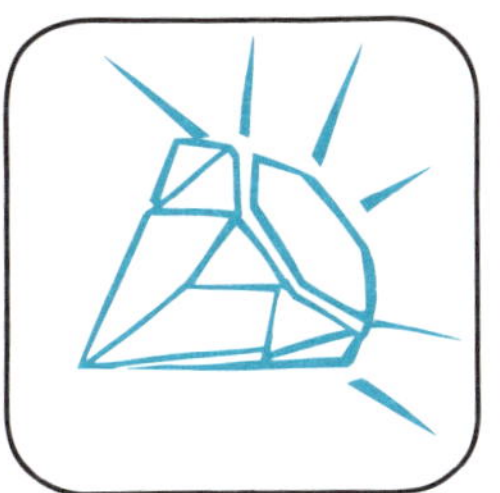

DIAMOND

The diamond is extraordinary because of its rarity, hardness, and beauty. The true diamond is Christ, for his hardness against temptation and suffering resulted in endurance. So martyrs and saints have been remembered as diamonds, faithful and true.

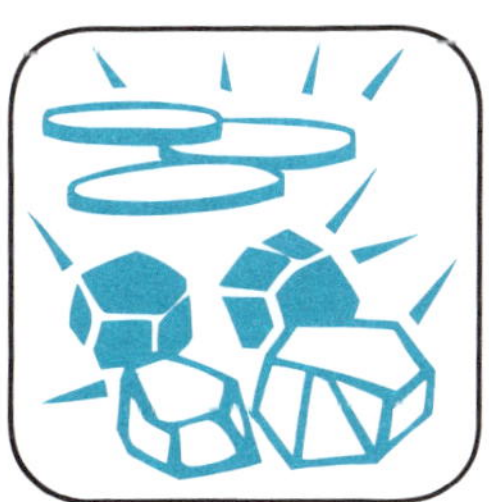

GOLD, SILVER

As a beautiful and valuable metal, gold is a symbol of divine perfection and of eternity. Gold backgrounds for paintings and icons designate heavenly light. In biblical times silver enjoyed the same status as gold and thus symbolizes divine perfection and beauty. Moreover, its brightness, especially after the refining process, suggests clarity and purity.

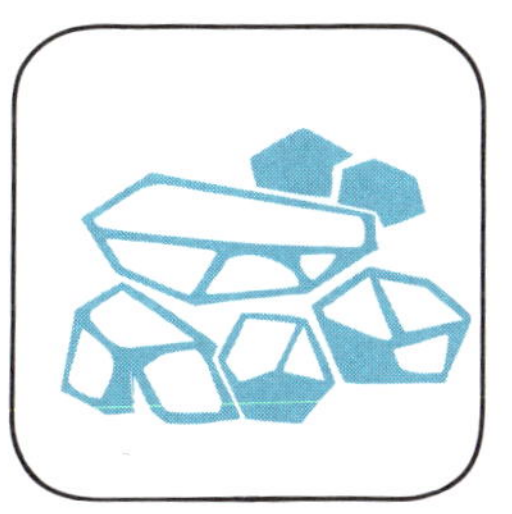

ROCK, STONE

Rocks and stones symbolize the divine because they are hard, strong, unchangeable, and enduring. God was often regarded as a rock. Messianic hopes in the Old Testament were tied to the cornerstone, which was later identified as Christ. The emerging building metaphor soon portrayed all Christians as stones, together constituting the church.

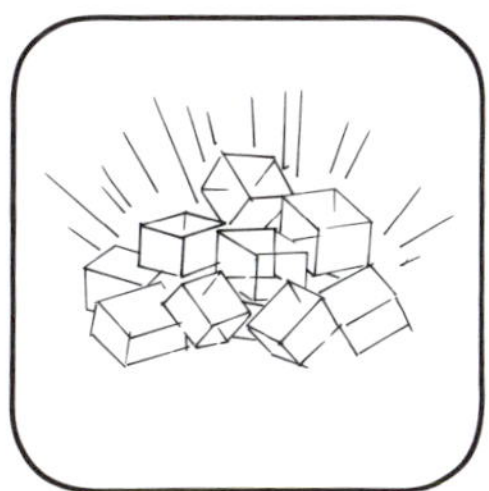

SALT

Like bread, salt was held to be essential to life. Jesus referred to his disciples as the "salt of the earth," essential to its well-being.

KEYS

One or two keys, the symbol for power or status, represent the apostle Peter, since he and his colleagues were given the authority to bind and loose sins on earth. Entrance to eternal life is via Jesus as the key himself.

STAFF

A single long staff is a tool or symbol of a shepherd. A staff with a crook symbolizes a spiritual shepherd. The staff anciently meant protective power as well as authority to work miraculous deeds. Most often Jesus is depicted as the Good Shepherd who holds the staff.

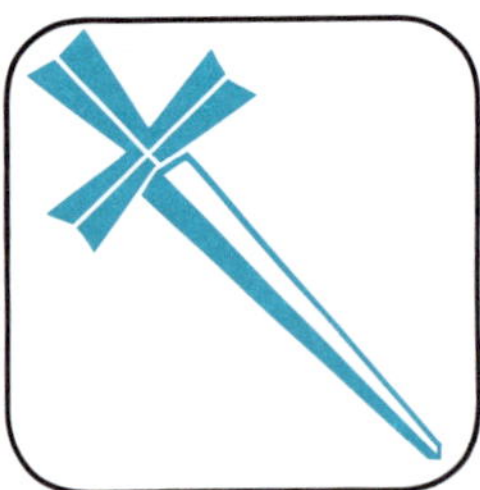

SWORD

As an implement of battle and war the sword denotes might. From might comes authority for making judgments. A two-edged sword stresses judgment and is meant to lift up Jesus as the ultimate judge over life and death. Jesus carries out his task through the Word, both Law and Gospel, the two edges of the sword. The sword is also a symbol of martyrdom.

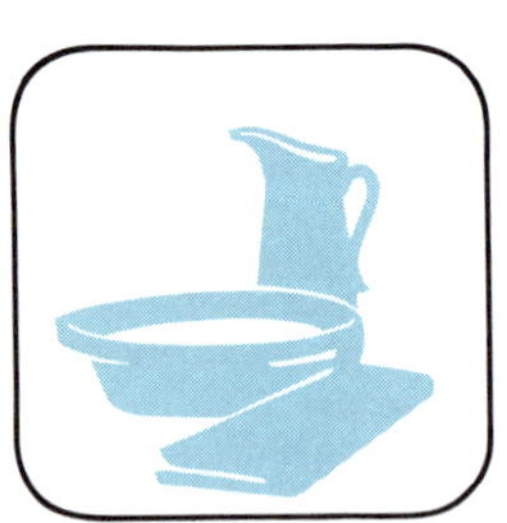

TOWEL, EWER, BASIN

Individually and together these three items have to do with washing and therefore symbolize cleanliness or purity. Opportunities for washing are offered to guests as a sign of hospitality. Jesus, washing the feet of his disciples on Maundy Thursday, turned cleanliness into loving service. Hence towel, ewer, and basin also symbolize ministry.

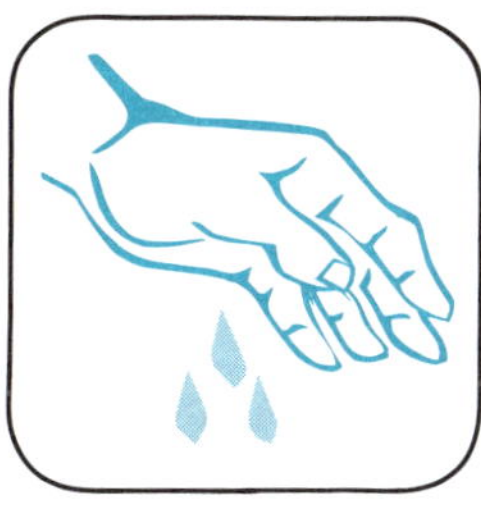

BLOOD

Blood is the symbol of life, especially of that life offered or gained through sacrifice. For most ancient cultures blood was thought to be or to contain life, so taking the blood of creatures and giving it to a deity signified a noteworthy offering. The shedding of Christ's blood is the ultimate sacrifice, commemorated in Holy Communion and depicted symbolically with drops flowing from the crucified Christ or from a wounded lamb.

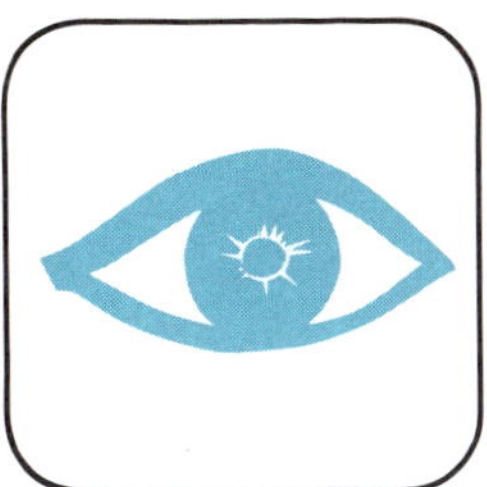

EYE

The eye symbolizes watchfulness either for protection or for care. Combined with a triangle it symbolizes the watchfulness of the Trinity. The eye is also used as the gate to the soul, thus a symbol of enlightenment.

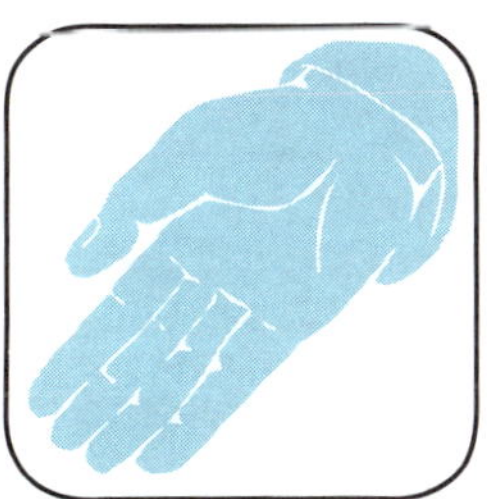

HAND, FINGER, ARM

Since the hand is essential to many kinds of human work, creativity, and care, it serves as a symbol of one's self. Hands are joined to experience spiritual contact with another. Blessing is transmitted through the laying on of a hand or hands. The right hand or an extended right arm stands for presence with power. A hand pointing downward with two fingers extended symbolizes creative presence.

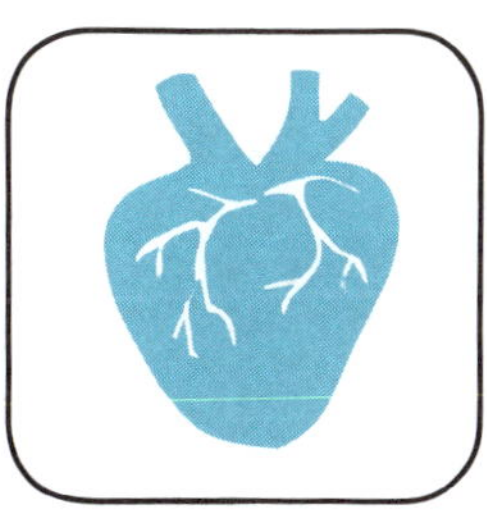

HEART

Some envision the heart to be the center of the human body, so it has become the symbol of love, deep feelings, or religious feelings.

MUSICAL INSTRUMENTS

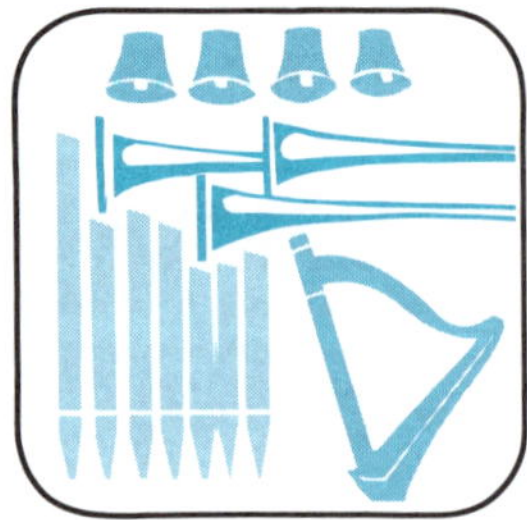

In general music is a symbol of heavenly joy, but various instruments have their own nuances of expression. Bells, with their acoustical carrying power, symbolize the evangelizing voice of God while a bird call suggests the freedom of the gospel. A flute evokes visions of pastoral scenes, the harp suggests heavenly music, and organ pipes symbolize festivity and praise. The trumpet is used to symbolize both judgment and proclamation.

COLORS

The present scheme of liturgical colors derives from a pattern established in the twelfth century, though its roots reach back to the time of Christ. As Christians are open to the color associations of diverse peoples of the world, color schemes in church symbolism continue to undergo change.

BLUE, which represents truth, is the color of the clear sky and of water, and is thus also a symbol of purity. Its use during Advent is meant to elicit hope in God's truth; in royal shades, blue heralds the coming of the King.

GOLD is the symbol of Jesus' resurrection.

WHITE originates in undiminished light, and therefore implies the eternal presence of God. By extension it also symbolizes heaven, purity, lordship, joy, glory, and celebration. White surrounded major moments of salvation.

PURPLE and **VIOLET** symbolize royalty since important secular leaders wore vestments made in these colors. Reddish hues reminded Christians of the blood shed by their King. In this way purple and violet came to be the choice for Lent and for penitential times.

GREEN is the color of vegetation, growth, spring, and also of hope. In liturgical usage it symbolizes growth, and specifies that time in between known as regular days. It is used for most Sundays in the Epiphany season and the season after Pentecost.

As the color of fire, **RED** symbolizes warmth, energy, desire, love, and commitment. It is used for Pentecost, and for other observances related to the Holy Spirit, such as ordination and the dedication of a church building. It is also the color of blood and thus symbolizes sacrifice, suffering, and martyrdom.

Deep red or **SCARLET** is often used for Palm/Passion Sunday and days following to combine royalty with the shedding of blood.

BLACK is used to symbolize death and grief. Liturgically, black can be used on Good Friday, though the absence of any color or furnishings more adequately conveys the emptiness of the day. Black is also used for Ash Wednesday when it symbolizes human death.

COMPOUND SYMBOLS

PERSONS OF THE TRINITY

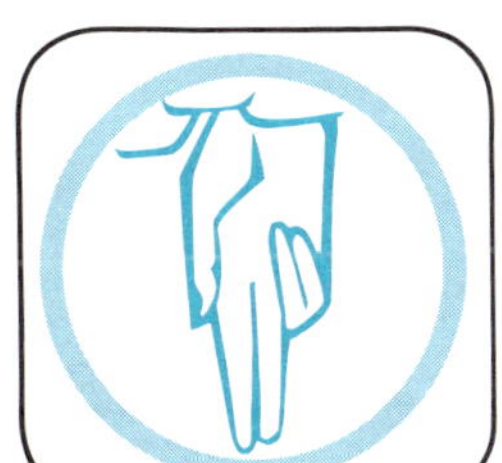

GOD THE FATHER

This common symbol, showing God's blessing and protection, is formed by placing a hand within a circular nimbus.

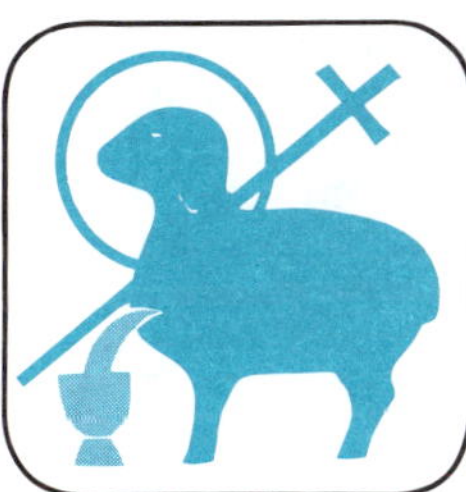

GOD THE SON

Five simple symbols have been used to form this symbol of Jesus: lamb, staff cross, nimbus, blood, and chalice. Together they express the sacrificial death of God's son, Jesus.

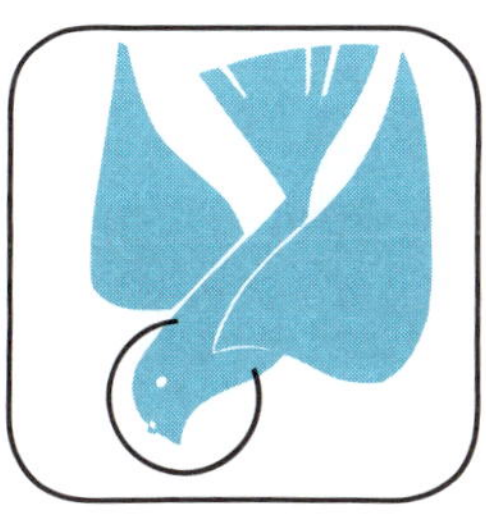

GOD THE SPIRIT

One of the most familiar symbols of the Holy Spirit combines the dove with the nimbus.

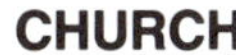

CHURCH

When a ship, a place of refuge, is portrayed with a mast shaped like a cross it is usually understood to be the church. A ship with a rainbow recalls God's promises to Noah and his family and God's deliverance through water and the ark.

THE CHRISTMAS CYCLE

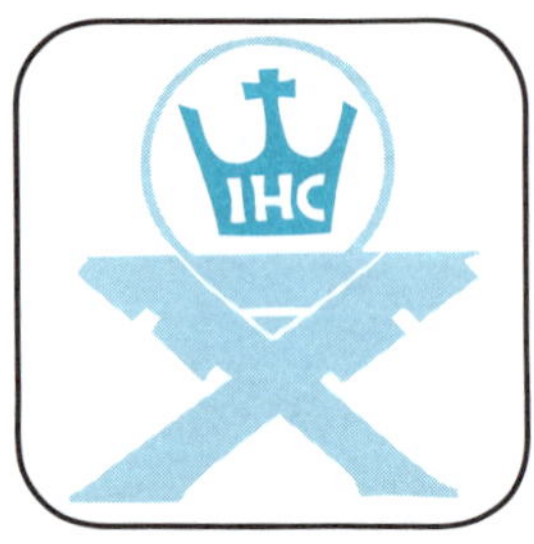

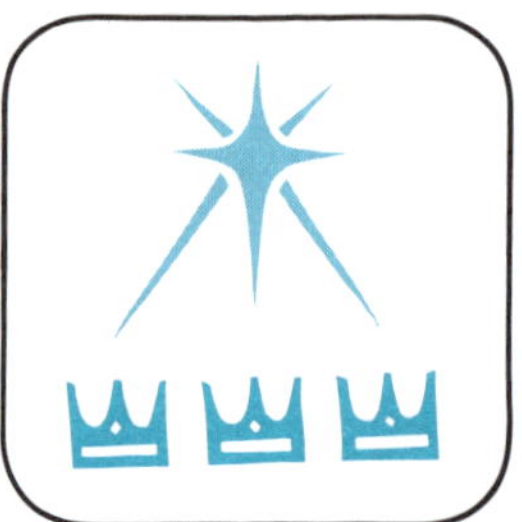

ADVENT SEASON • Inspiration for this combination of sun and the Chi-Rho derives from a favorite Advent text, Malachi 4:2, where Christ is referred to as "the sun of righteousness."

CHRISTMAS SEASON • A simple manger receives elaboration through the additions of a crown, symbol of authority and power; a nimbus; and the popular monogram, ihc, in order to underline the significance of the incarnation.

EPIPHANY SEASON • The epiphany star led the Magi, thought to be kings, to the side of Jesus. Rays from the star are meant to suggest continuing light for generations to come.

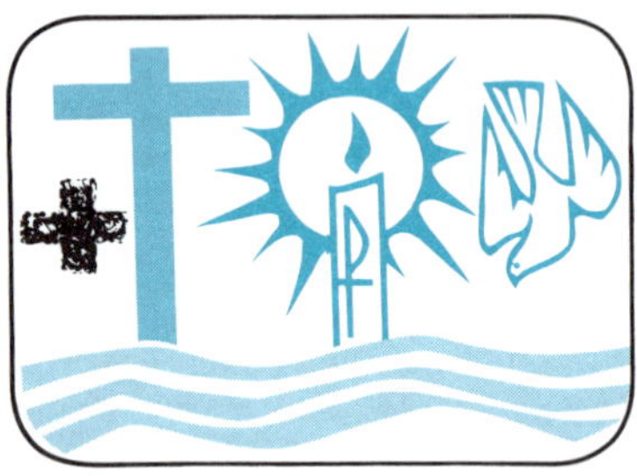

THE EASTER CYCLE

Because Jesus' death and resurrection constitute God's most complete saving action for humankind, the seasons of Lent and Easter can be understood as a unit. One compound symbol draws on many rivers of experience: the ashen black cross from Ash Wednesday, the waters of Baptism, the Latin cross of Good Friday, the light of the paschal candle, the resurrected Sun which is Jesus, and the coming of the Spirit.

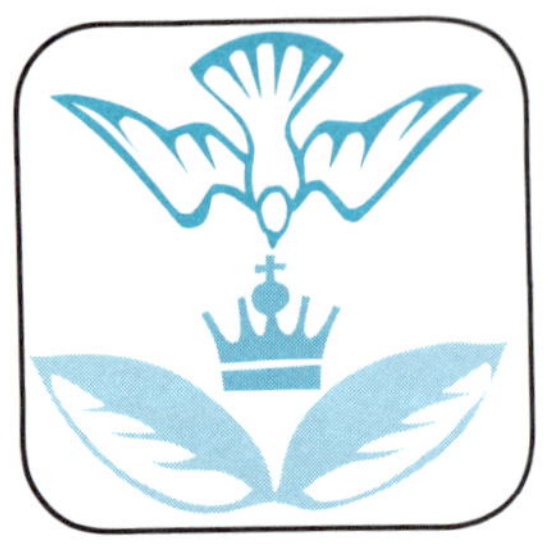

THE TIME OF THE CHURCH

THE SEASON AFTER PENTECOST

The Sundays after Pentecost, concluding with Christ the King, are for growth and faith within the church, through the power of the Spirit.

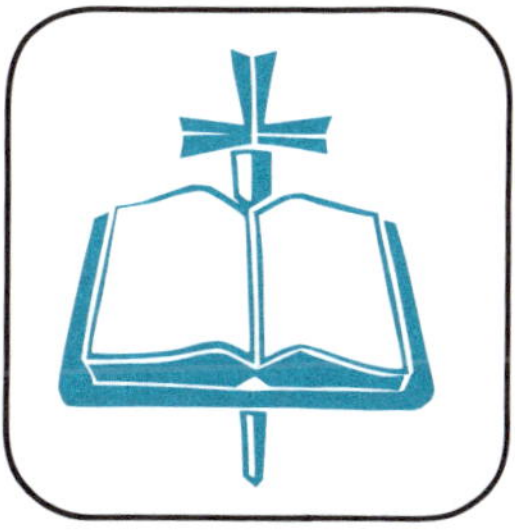

WORD OF GOD • The book is open, which indicates the usefulness of the Word of God, a point emphasized by the addition of the "sword of the Spirit," which comes from Ephesians 6:17.

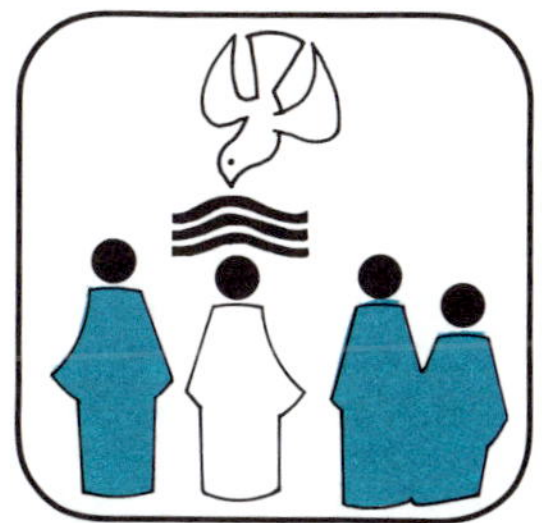

BAPTISM • This presentation begins to unveil the richness of God's saving action in Baptism: living water, the assembly, light, monarchy of God (staff cross), new life (white baptismal garment), and the Holy Spirit (dove).

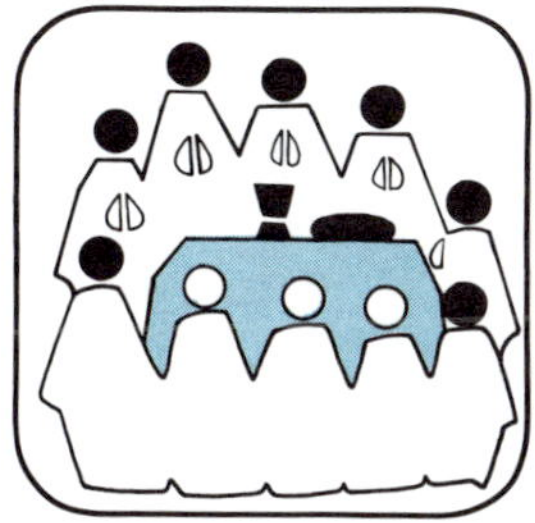

LORD'S SUPPER • Combined here are some of the symbols integral to the Lord's Supper: chalice, bread, assembly, eating a meal, and the circle of fullness.

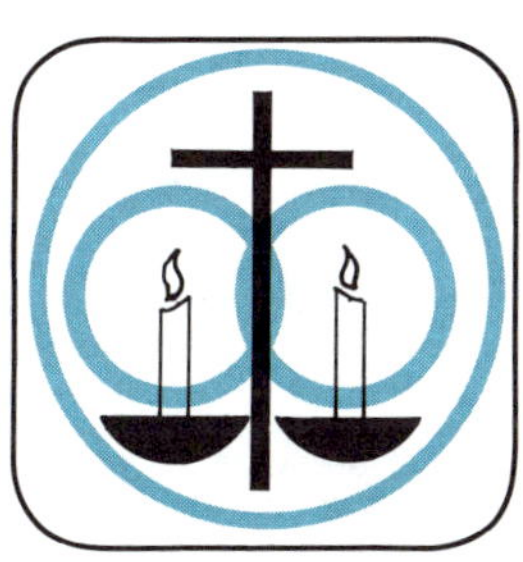

MARRIAGE • Two interlocking circles or rings symbolize the unity of individuals whose identities are centered in the burning light of Christ in each. Their unity is in a circle, backed by Christ, indicated by the Latin cross, who outlasts their own relationship with each other.

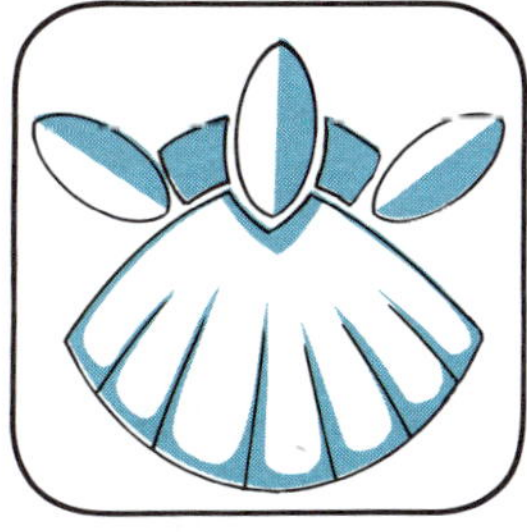

AFFIRMATION OF BAPTISM • The leaves of a plant within a baptismal scallop shell symbolize the growth of baptismal faith, which is ongoing but affirmed at significant moments of one's life.

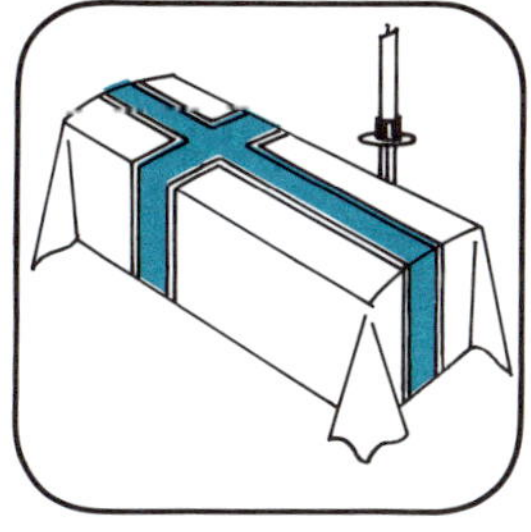

BURIAL • A white pall over a casket signifies the lasting power of Baptism even in death. The light of the paschal candle symbolizes the unending life in Christ for baptized Christians.

TERMS: SANCTUARY FURNISHINGS

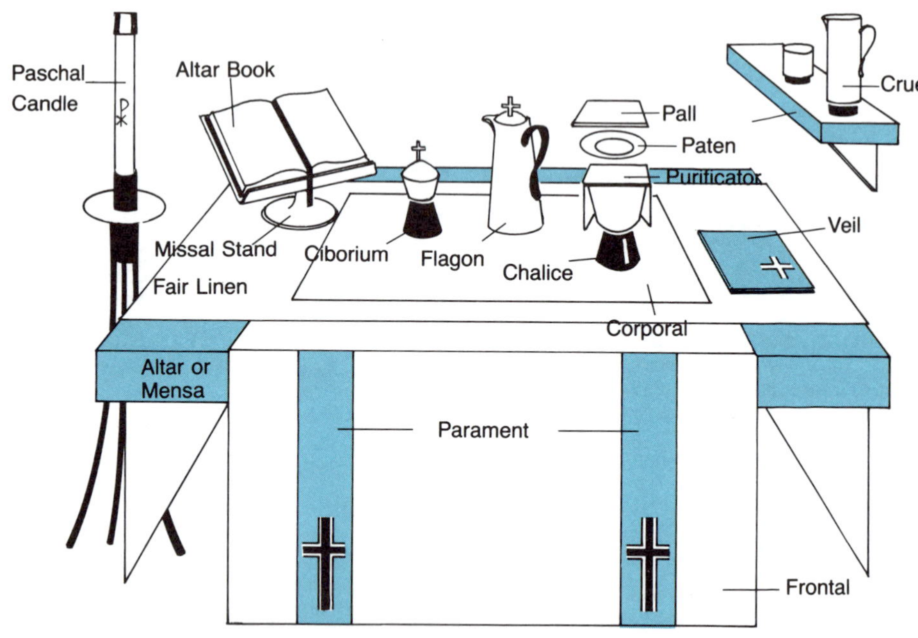

ALTAR BOOK • The service book in large type that contains the text of the liturgy of the church.

CHALICE • Vessel or cup that holds the wine for Holy Communion.

CIBORIUM • A chalice-shaped vessel with lid used for the storage of bread for Holy Communion.

CORPORAL • A square of white linen placed centrally on the mensa, on which bread and wine are set for Holy Communion.

CRUET • A glass vessel for storing wine or water for the celebration of Holy Communion.

FAIR LINEN • The top or final cloth covering the mensa. It is made from white linen, often with five embroidered crosses.

FLAGON • A storage vessel usually made of metal from which wine is poured into the chalice for Holy Communion.

FRONTAL • A parament, in the liturgical color, that extends across the face of the altar from the mensa to the floor.

MISSAL STAND • Book stand or cushion on which the altar book is placed.

PALL • A stiff, white, linen-covered square used to cover the chalice.

PARAMENT • A cloth covering, in a liturgical color, used to adorn altar, pulpit, lectern, or ambo.

PASCHAL CANDLE • A large, white candle symbolizing the resurrected Christ, lit for the Easter season, Baptisms, and funerals.

PATEN • The plate used to hold the bread during celebrations of Holy Communion.

PURIFICATOR • A square linen napkin used to cleanse the rim of the chalice during the distribution of Holy Communion.

VEIL • A cloth placed over sacramental vessels before and after Holy Communion. The chalice veil is a specialized veil in liturgical colors.

TERMS: WORSHIP SPACE

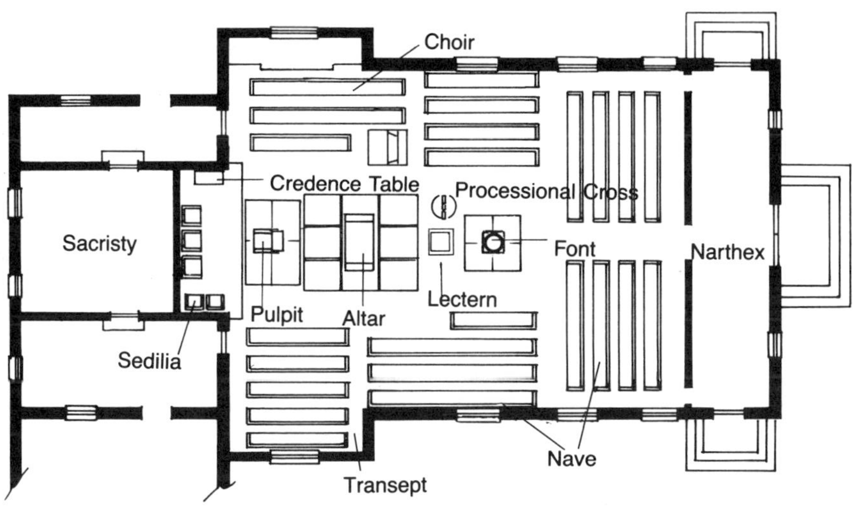

ALTAR • The table used for the celebration of Holy Communion. It is the focal point of the worship space.

CHANCEL • The raised area at the front of the church building. The space for altar and pulpit or ambo.

CHOIR • A group of singers, or the place where the choir and other clergy sit; traditionally the part of the church between the nave and sanctuary.

CREDENCE • A side table or shelf used for the storage of eucharistic elements, paraments, vessels, offering plates, or other equipment for a liturgy.

FONT • A pool or receptacle of water for Holy Baptism.

LECTERN • A reading stand in full view of the people from which the lessons or prayers are read.

NARTHEX • Entrance area that provides transition from the outside to the nave.

NAVE • The body of a church building between the narthex and the chancel; where the pews or chairs are located.

PROCESSIONAL CROSS • A cross or crucifix on a staff carried at the head of a procession.

PULPIT • A raised enhanced reading desk generally used for preaching and the reading of the Gospel when it is read from a desk.

SACRISTY • Room for the storage of vestments, vessels, and paraments and for vesting and preparation by the worship leaders.

SANCTUARY • Section of the worship space directly surrounding the altar.

SEDILIA • Seats for the worship leaders.

TRANSEPT • The transverse part of a traditional church building that is at a right angle to the nave.

INDEX